How To Play Chess For Beginners: Tips & Strategies To Win At Chess

Joe Carlton

Learn more about chess at
www.chessblog.info

D1315328

Chess symbols

x	capture
+	check
++	double check
#	checkmate
=	draw, equality, promotes to
!	good move
!!	excellent move
?	bad move
??	blunder
!?	interesting move
?!	dubious move
ep	en passant
0-0, 0-0-0	castle kingside, castle queenside
+/=	white is slightly better
=/+	black is slightly better
+/-	white is clearly better
-/+	black is clearly better
+-	white is winning
-+	black is winning
1-0	white won
0-1	black won
½-½	game was drawn

CONTENTS

Introduction

Chess has been around for about 1500 years and most likely originated in India just before the 6th century AD. From there, it was passed onto many other countries like Persia, through the entire Arab World, Europe, Asia and eventually everywhere else around the world. Chess is truly one of the most recognizable games in the world, despite what some people may think of it, and has been played by people coming from all walks of life from peasants to royalty.

More recently, chess has been used as a brain training tool for kids or as way to learn about business strategies. This may be true to some extent but I can assure you that most people who play chess don't play chess because they want to improve their business acumen or help improve their children's school performance.

Most people play chess because they enjoy it and can engage in mental warfare, or a contest of intelligence if you will, with their opponents.

This book was written to help teach those interested in learning more about chess, including the basic rules, basic strategies and tips to get better at chess quickly.

So if you're ready to learn more about the royal game that has stood the test of time, then read on.

The Basic Rules

In the game of chess, there are 32 pieces, 16 for the white side and 16 for the black side. The chessboard is a square checkered board of 64 alternating light and dark squares. Some chessboards may also have chess notation written on the sides of it and some may not.
The starting position of a chess game is as follows:

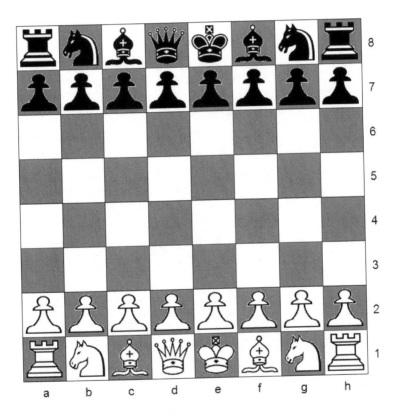

To always setup a board correctly, remember "white on the right" which means that the square on the right hand side must be white (in this case, the h1 square).
The queens start on the square of their color. In other words, the white queen starts on a white square and the black queen starts on the black square.
Also remember that the kings must face each other.

To name a square, simply find the letter notation and pair it with the corresponding number notation. As just recently demonstrated, the lower right hand corner of the board is the square h1.
The pieces are:
PAWN

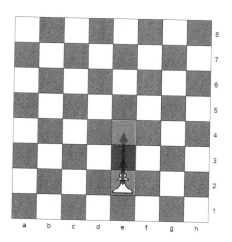

A pawn can move either 1 or 2 squares from its starting position. Pawns cannot move backwards

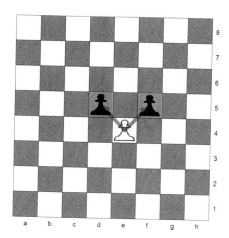

Pawns can only capture diagonally

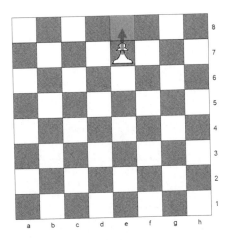

When pawns reach the back rank, they can be promoted to any of the following pieces below

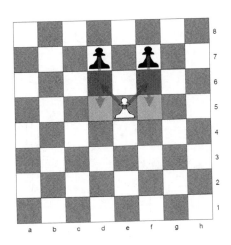

When black plays either of the pawns onto the green squares, white can capture them as shown. This is called "en passant". Black can also do this as shown below

KNIGHT

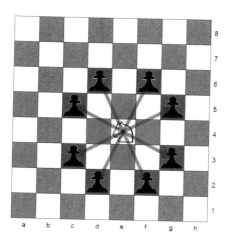

You can remember how it moves by the shape of the knight which looks like the letter L. For example, the knight above can move to and capture any of the 8 pawns highlighted in red. The knight can also jump over friendly and enemy troops.

BISHOP

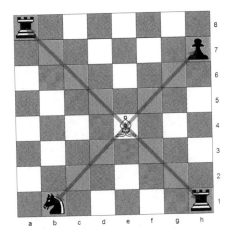

The bishop moves diagonally and can only move on 1 square color. For example, the bishop above can only move to any of the highlighted squares and also capture any of the black pieces. Bishops cannot jump over other pieces.

ROOK

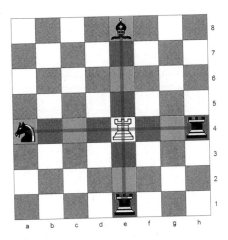

The rook moves across or up and down the board. For example, the white rook above can move to any of the highlighted squares and capture any of the black pieces. It cannot jump over other pieces.

QUEEN

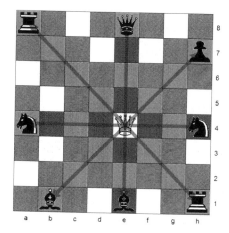

The queen has the combined power of a rook and a bishop. For example, the white queen above can capture any of the black pieces. It cannot jump over other pieces.

KING

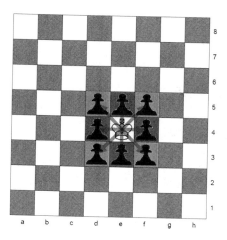

The king can only move 1 square at a time and in any direction. The king can only capture a piece if it does not lead to the king getting checked. The king cannot jump over other pieces. Along with the rook, the king can also perform a move called "castling". Under standard chess rules, the king cannot be captured.

Quick quiz: In this position, how many pawns can the white king legally capture?

"Special" moves

<u>En passant</u> (pronounced "on-pass-ont") – a move that allows a pawn to capture another pawn without having to directly attack it

Conditions of en passant
En passant can only be done by a pawn and only when the opponent's pawn has move 2 squares from its starting position.

<u>Castling</u> – a move that allows the king to move 2 squares and the corresponding rook to move directly adjacent to the king on the opposite side at the same time

Conditions of castling
Castling can't be performed if:
-   The king has already moved
-   The rook that you want to castle with has already moved
-   One of the squares that the king passes through is blockaded or will allow the king to be checked

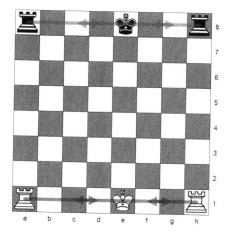

In this position, either white or black can castle on either the kingside (squares from e1 to h1 and e8 to h8) or queenside (squares from d1 to a1 or d8 to a8).

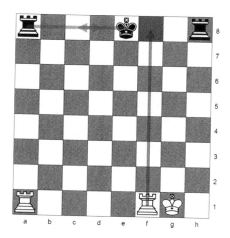

In this position, white has castled kingside. By doing so, white's rook controls the f8 square and prevents black from castling kingside otherwise

black's king will be checked.
However, black is still allowed to
castle, but on the queenside instead

The chess pieces are assigned a value to them in order to give a rough idea as to who has the advantage. For example, if you have capture more pawns than your opponent, then you are said to have a material advantage. If both sides have captured a similar amount of material, then it could be said that neither side has the advantage, and the position is about equal.

Here is the point system with the English algebraic notation:

Pawn (no abbreviation)   1 point

Knight (N)   3 points

Bishop (B)   3.5 points

Rook (R)   5 points

Queen (Q)   9 points

King (K)   priceless

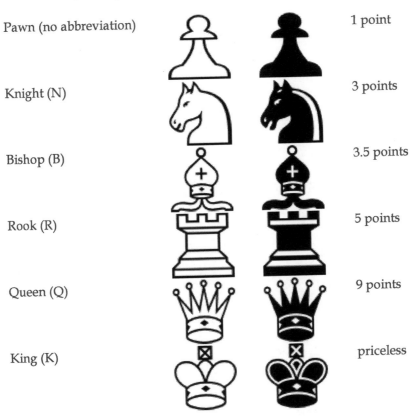

In some other books, you may read that a bishop is worth 3 points as well, which is the same as the knight and some other books may even say that it is worth 4 points. Bishops are better than knights in most situations but due to it being limited on the same square color and not being able to jump over pieces, it is only slightly better than a knight.

If you happen to read some old chess books, they use descriptive notation which is very rarely used these days because it's not as simple or intuitive as the modern day algebraic notation. But if you would like to read the games of the past in these old books, then here's the notation for that:

P: pawn

Kt or N: knight

B: bishop

R: rook

Q: queen

K: king

To denote a square, you must state it in relation to what the starting piece file is on and the rank number from the perspective of the player. For example, 1. P-K4 is the first move with the pawn on the king's file, moving it to the 4th rank from white's point of view. Essentially, this translates to 1. e4 in today's notation. Another example is 2 … R6xN which is black's second move with the rook on the 6th rank from black's point of view taking the only white knight within its range. Notice also how the old notation uses the dash sign (-) to indicate a piece is "moving to" some square.

Also:

- White always moves first (for chess pieces that are not traditionally black and white, the lighter colored side moves first)
- Players can only make 1 move at a time
- You cannot capture your own pieces
- You cannot pass (at least not directly)
- "Touch move" means that once you touch a piece, you must move it (usually only in tournament conditions). This doesn't apply if you say that you are "adjusting" the piece or if you say "j'adoube" (pronounced "zha-doob")

General chess etiquette involves shaking the opponent's hand before playing and wishing them luck. Of course, this is purely optional but is good practice if you want to play in tournaments.

If you'd like to know the complete set of rules for competitive chess, then you can visit http://rules.fide.com/

Chess Language

Over the years, chess jargon has been developed to help communicate certain ideas across. Some examples are:

rank - a row of squares from one end of the board to the other

back rank – the 8th rank for white or the 1st rank for black

file - a column of squares from one end of the board to the other

diagonal – a diagonal of squares (eg bishops move along diagonals) from one end of the board to the other

check - this is a move that places the king under attack

checkmate, aka mate - this is a check that the king cannot escape or parry and because of this, ends the game (shah mat - persian for 'the king is dead')

stalemate - this is a position whereby the player to move cannot make any legal moves and is not in check

fork - a tactic that attacks more than 1 piece

double attack - a tactic that attacks 2 pieces (a double attack made by the same piece can also be called a fork)

pin - a tactic that makes it unfavourable or illegal to move a piece as the more valuable piece behind will be under attack

skewer - a tactic similar to a pin but the more valuable piece in front of the less valuable piece

castle (as a verb), castling - to perform the castling move

clearance – a tactic that allows a piece to be able to move to squares that were previously inaccessible

blunder – a very bad move that will likely lead to a losing position or throws away a winning advantage

blitz – a fast game, usually 5 minutes per side

hanging - undefended

exchange - to capture an enemy piece and in turn allow the opponent to capture back (not the same as an exchange up/down, exchange advantage)

an exchange up/down - an exchange up is to have an enemy rook for the price of a knight or bishop, to be an exchange down is losing a rook for a knight or a bishop sacrifice, often abbreviated to sac - to deliberately lose a valuable piece (most famously, the queen) in order gain an immediate or long-term advantage.

discovery - a tactic that uncovers an indirect attack against a piece (eg. discovered check - an indirect check, discovered attack)

double check - a move that places the king under attack twice (not the same as checkmate)

decoy/diversion/distraction/deflection - not really chess specific but you may come across it. It is exactly as it sounds, for eg a strategy to tempt or distract your opponent from your intended plan

material – pieces (not the king) and/or pawns

transpose – to turn into a similar or identical position

tempo – time or a move

undermine - a strategy that attacks the weakest point of something

prophylaxis - a strategy that maintains the balance of the position

development - piece deployment

promotion - when a pawn reaches the final rank it can be replaced with a more valuable piece (except the king)

x-ray – the umbrella term either referring to the pin and skewer used either as offense or defence

zugzwang – a position where any legal move leads to a bad position for the player to move

zwischenzug (aka intermediate move or in-between move) – a move that poses a threat large enough that forces a move (for example, a check) or if the move is ignored will result in a significant disadvantage

kibitz – to observe another chess game

patzer – a chess novice

grandmaster (often abbreviated to GM) – the highest title of chess, aside from world champion, that a player can receive (refer to the FIDE handbook for more information about international chess titles)

There are other terms but these are the ones you can keep in mind.

Note, throughout this chess book (and most chess books), the player who is playing white or black is often referred to as "he" or "his". This is not meant to be sexist or to deliberately exclude women, it just so happens that chess has traditionally been played mainly by men ever since it was created (and still to this day). So when you read "he" or "him", it really means "the player" in general.

You will also notice that chess tournament halls are fairly quiet areas, aside from the sound of chess pieces dropping on the board, the ticking of chess clocks and the shuffling of people. It is a rule in tournament chess that you are not allowed to speak to your opponent unless you are saying good luck before a game, adjusting a piece or offering a draw.

You are allowed to announce check and checkmate (and probably stalemate) but in common practice most players do not do this. Why? Because it's assumed that you should know when you are in check. Besides, it isn't very hard to spot one anyway, but it will take a little practice to get used to. Try friendly games first or games against the computer, since it will always announce check for you.

Basic Checkmates

There are several simple checkmates that you can practice. Here is the basic strategy for each:

<u>K & Q v. K</u> – the strategy is to gradually corner the enemy king with your queen until your opponent only has 2 squares left to move. Then move your king towards the enemy king and deliver checkmate. Just be careful of stalemate.

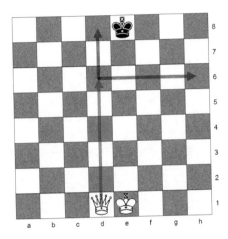

Qd6 – creates a box around the king

Eventually, you should corner in the

king like this so that it only has 2
squares to move on. Mate is threatened
on g7, d8 or e8, in this case

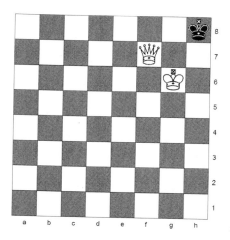

Not like this however, because this is
stalemate

This is also another stalemate to avoid.

K & 2R v. K – the strategy is to cut the king off file by file or rank by rank until you get checkmate. It's almost like a staircase pattern, cutting the king off rank by rank or file by file. The rooks can deliver checkmate without the help of the king.

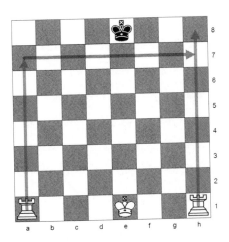

Ra7 followed by Rh8 mate

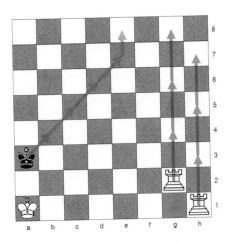

The "staircase mate" – 1. Rh3+, 2. Rg4+,
3. Rh5+, 4. Rg6+, 5. Rh7+, 6. Rg8#. But
there is a faster way to mate here.

K & R v. K – the strategy is similar to K & Q v K. You slowly box in the enemy king with your rook whilst protecting it with your king. Then deliver checkmate in the corner

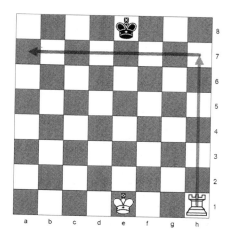

Rh7 – traps the king on the back rank

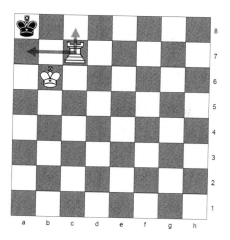

Then use the king and rook to slowly push the black king into the corner and deliver mate. In this case, Rc8#

K & 2B v. K – the strategy is to cut off the enemy king diagonally by using your king and 2B. Your king plays more of a role in boxing in the enemy king this time. Once in the corner, deliver mate.

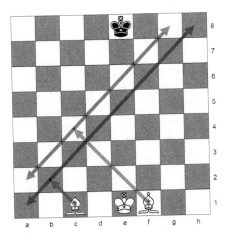

1. Bc4 then 2. Bb2 creates a diagonal barrier
that the black king cannot cross over

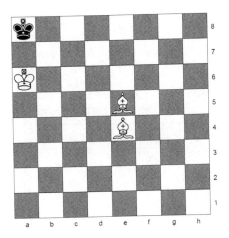

Then use the bishops and the king to close
in the black king by making the "triangular
box" smaller and smaller and then deliver
checkmate in the corner

<u>K & N + B v. K</u> – the strategy is to force the enemy king onto the file or rank at the edge of the board. This is the hardest part. Once you've forced the king onto the edge of the board, then create the setup, push the king into the corner of the same color as your bishop and deliver mate. If the king is already in the 'right' corner, then your job is simpler. Most beginners, and even some strong club players, have difficulty with this mate.

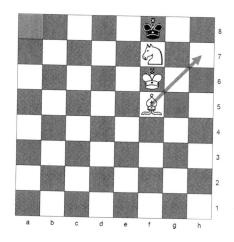

This is the setup. Notice how the white pieces are aligned with the black king. White's objective is to get the black king into the light squared corner so that he can deliver checkmate with the bishop. So white starts off with 1. Bh7

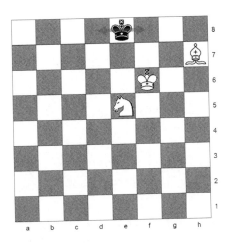

1...Ke8 2. Ne5 black can now decide to play either Kf8 back or try an escape with Kd8. Unfortunately for black, both moves fail.

If Black decides to play 2… Kd8 then 3. Ke6, Kc7 4. Nd7 (diagram 1), Kc6 5. Bd3! (this creates the cage or box to push the king into the corner), Kc7 6. Bb5!, Kb7 7. Kd6, Kb8 8. Kc7 (diagram 2 - as you can see, the black king is now trapped in a tiny little cage, very much like the K & Q v. K ending), Ka8 9. Nb6+, Ka7 10. Nc8+, Ka8 11. Bc6# (diagram 3)

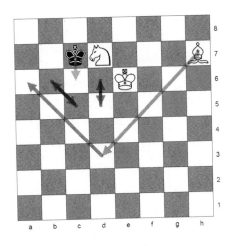

Diagram 1

Diagram 2

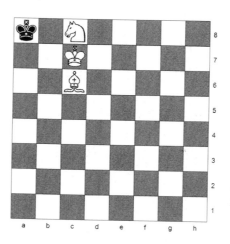

Diagram 3

Or, if Black plays 2...Kf8 instead then we can create the typical knight, king bishop setup to push the king into the "right" colored corner and deliver mate. 3. Nd7+, Ke8 4. Ke6, Kd8 5. Kd6, Ke8 6. Bg6+, Kd8 7. Bf7 (diagram 4 – notice how the black king is getting closer to the "right" square), Kc8 8. Nc5, Kd8 9. Nb7+, Kc8 10. Kc6, Kb8 11. Kb6, Kc8 12. Be6+, Kb8 (diagram 5– a familiar position, but now mate is in the air) 13. Bd7, Ka8 14. Nc5, Kb8 15. Na6+, Ka8 16. Bc6# (diagram 6)

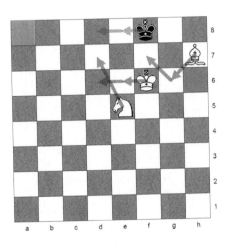

White plans Nd7+ then Ke6, Kd6, Bg6 and Bf7

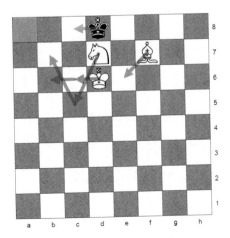

Diagram 4

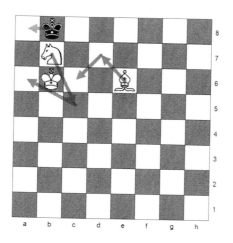

Diagram 5

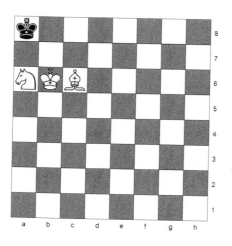

Diagram 6

This endgame will take some time to master, but it's quite rewarding once you do. Try and play it against a very strong opponent and see if you can checkmate that person in less than 50 moves starting from the centre of the board, like so:

Practice position

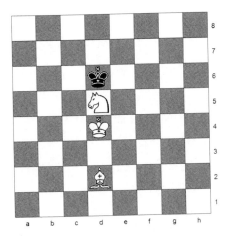

Quick question, which corner do you have to push the king into in order to checkmate your opponent?

Some other positions will be covered in the endgame section.

Just for your interest K & 2N v K is a draw unless the weaker side has a pawn or some kind of material, then the side with 2 knights may be able to checkmate. For example, if the weaker side has an extra pawn, then the strategy is to push the enemy king into the corner, create the stalemate pattern. This would force the weaker side into to play the pawn due to zugzwang, which would allow the side with 2 knights to deliver checkmate.

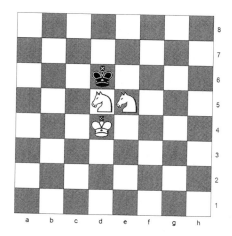

This position is surprisingly a draw. Despite having 2 knights, it is not legally possible for white to force checkmate. Try it out for yourself.

However, the position below is a win for white.

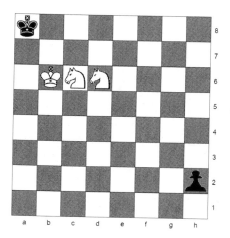

1.Nb5 h1=Q (forced due to zugzwang) 2.Nc7#. If the black pawn wasn't there, then white couldn't checkmate black and the black king would be in stalemate.

Openings

How you open the game, as white or black, is really up to your playing style. Most chess openings are "playable" (playable means that if you played a certain opening or series of moves accurately, it is unlikely to lead you to have a bad or inferior position), whereas some are a little dubious and a few have been refuted outright. If you stick to the most popular openings, then you should be fine. This is the best advice when you start out learning chess and that is to stick to what is well known.

After you've gained some experience, then you try out less popular openings. These openings often have traps early on and can be used to catch your opponents by surprise. But against stronger players, they probably won't work so just be mindful of that when you play. Here are some of the most common openings played. Check out this link http://en.chessbase.com/post/popularity-of-chess-openings-over-time for more information.

Ruy Lopez (pronounced roo-ee lopez, also known as the **Spanish opening**)

1.e4 e5 2.Nf3 Nc6 3.Bb5

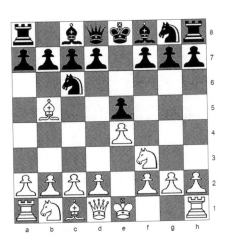

Sicilian Defence

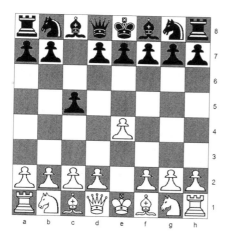

1.e4 c5

Queen's Gambit Declined (often abbreviated to QGD)

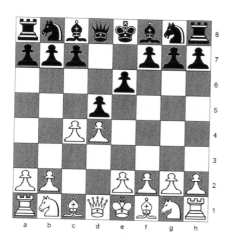

1.d4 d5 2.c4 e6

Slav Defence

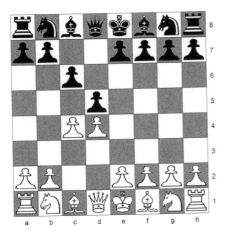

1.d4 d5 2.c4 c6

Nimzo-Indian Defence

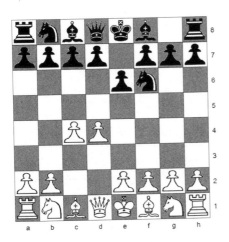

1.d4 Nf6 2.c4 e6

French Defence

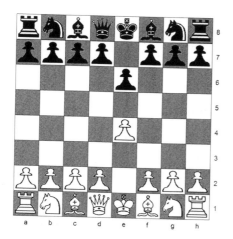

1.e4 e6

These are the most common openings that you'll see in tournament practice.

Club Level Openings

Here are some lesser known openings that are often played at club level. These openings are often played in order to avoid or sidestep huge amounts of opening theory from the so-called "main openings" as described above.

Alekhine Defence

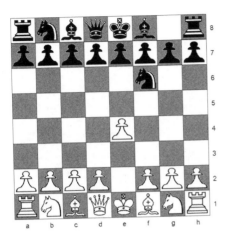

1.e4 Nf6

Scandanavian Defence (also known as the centre counter attack. It also seems to violate the basic rule that you shouldn't bring your queen out too early, but in this opening, this is an exception)

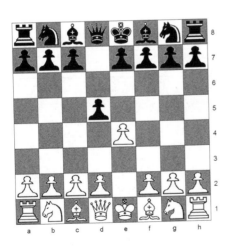

1.e4 d5

Caro-Kann Defence

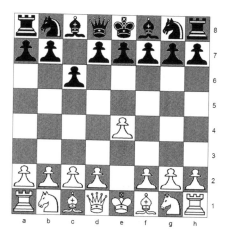

1.e4 c6

Modern Opening

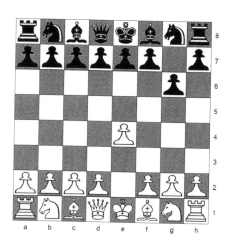

1.e4 g6

Pirc Opening (note the modern and pirc openings often transpose into one another, so the opening ideas are very similar)

1.e4 d6

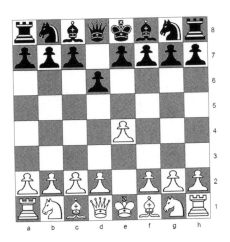

Nf3 Opening (doesn't really have a name, some refer to as a Reti or Zukertort opening, since it can transpose into many other openings. Keeps an opponent guessing about what you're about to play)

1.Nf3

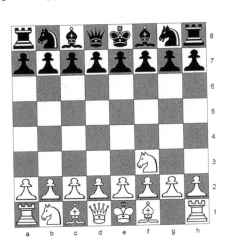

English Opening (an opening with highly drawish tendencies)

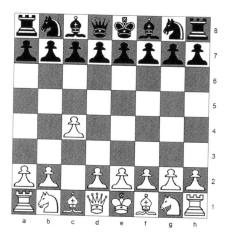

1.c4

Grandmaster Openings

Also, here are some of the openings played at grandmaster level

Catalan Opening

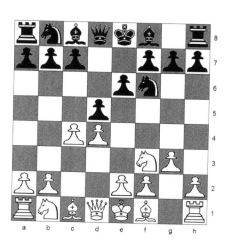

1.d4 d5 2.c4 e6 3.Nf3 Nf6 4.g3

(the first 2 moves are the same as QGD but what makes this a Catalan is that white plays g3)

Grünfeld Defence

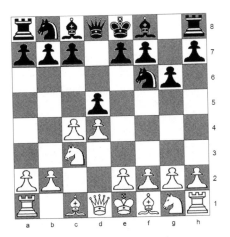

1.d4 Nf6 2.c4 g6 3.Nc3 d5

Berlin Defence (best example is when Kramnik used this to defeat Kasparov in the world championship in 2000 and was also used just last year in the 2013 world championship where Carlsen defeated Anand in game 6 with this opening)

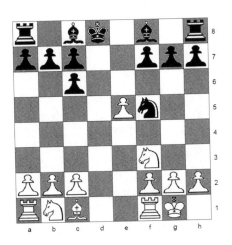

1.e4 e5 2.Nf3 Nc6 3.Bb5 Nf6 4.O-O Nxe4 5.d4 Nd6 6.Bxc6 dxc6 7.dxe5 Nf5 8.Qxd8+ Kxd8

King's Indian Defence (not seen so commonly anymore, but was once Garry Kasparov's preferred opening as black. Despite being a queen pawn opening, this opening is very sharp and tactical)

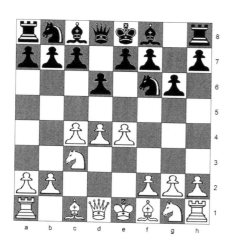

1.d4 Nf6 2.c4 g6 3.Nc3 d6 4.e4

There are hundreds of other lesser played openings and sidelines, which would not be possible to cover in this book alone. For these openings, you should play according to general strategies, which are to develop quickly, control the centre, don't waste time and get your king to safety. Of course, it helps if you know 1 or 2 lines just in case you don't fall in a cheap opening trap.

Opening Traps

Speaking of opening traps, here are some traps that might be useful to you:

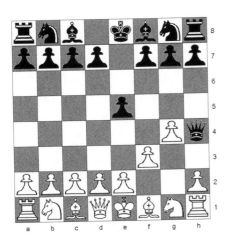

The 2 move checkmate (aka Fool's mate) – the shortest legal checkmate in chess

1.f3 e5 2.g4 Qh4# 0-1

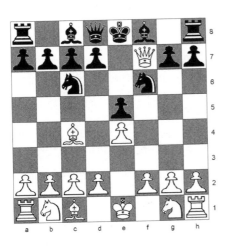

The (in)famous 4 move checkmate

1.e4 e5 2.Bc4 Nc6 3.Qh5 Nf6 4.Qxf7# 1-0

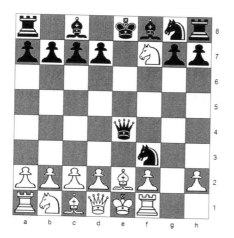

Blackburne-Shilling Trap

1.e4 e5 2.Nf3 Nc6 3.Bc4
Nd4 4.Nxe5 Qg5 5.Nxf7
Qxg2 6.Rf1 Qxe4+ 7.Be2
Nf3# 0-1

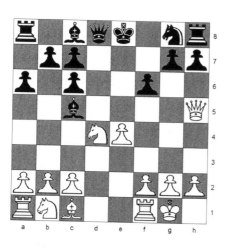

A simple Ruy Lopez Exchange trap

1.e4 e5 2.Nf3 Nc6 3.Bb5
a6 4.Bxc6 dxc6 5.O-O f6
6.d4 exd4 7.Nxd4 Bc5
8.Qh5+ followed by 9.
Qxc5+- winning a piece

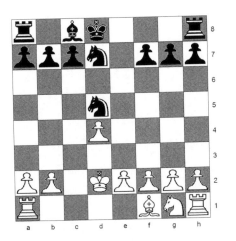

Elephant trap

1.d4 d5 2.c4 e6 3.Nc3 Nf6
4.Bg5 Nbd7 5.cxd5 exd5
6.Nxd5?? Nxd5! 7.Bxd8
Bb4+ 8.Qd2 Bxd2+
9.Kxd2 Kxd8-+ and
Black is up a full piece

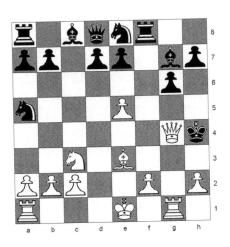

Fischer's trap

1.e4 c5 2.Nf3 Nc6 3.d4
cxd4 4.Nxd4 g6 5.Nc3
Bg7 6.Be3 Nf6 7.Bc4 O-O
8.Bb3 Na5 9.e5 Ne8
10.Bxf7+!! Kxf7 (better
would be 10… Kh8)
11.Ne6! Kxe6 (if 11…
dxe6 then 12. Qxd8 wins
the queen) 12.Qd5+ Kf5
13.g4+ Kxg4 14.Rg1+
Kh5 15.Qd1+ Kh4
16.Qg4#

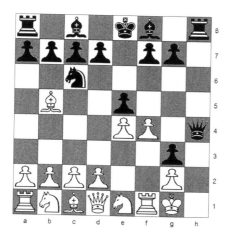

Fishing pole trap

1.e4 e5 2.Nf3 Nc6 3.Bb5 Nf6 4.O-O Ng4 5.h3 h5 6.hxg4?? hxg4 7.Ne1 Qh4 8.f4 g3 and black mates in 1.

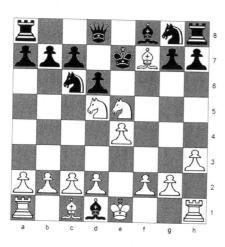

Legal's mate (an old trap)

1.e4 e5 2.Nf3 Nc6 3.Bc4 d6 4.Nc3 Bg4 5.h3 Bh5 6.Nxe5 Bxd1?? (if 6…Nxe5 then 7. Qxh5, Nxc4 8. Qb5+ followed by Qxc4 with a pawn up) 7.Bxf7+ Ke7 8.Nd5# 1-0

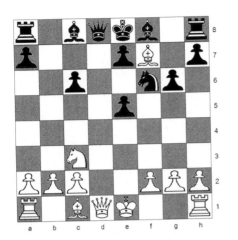

Magnus smith trap

1.e4 c5 2.Nf3 d6 3.d4
cxd4 4.Nxd4 Nf6 5.Nc3
Nc6 6.Bc4 g6 7.Nxc6
bxc6 8.e5 dxe5 9.Bxf7+ +-
followed by Qxd8
winning the queen

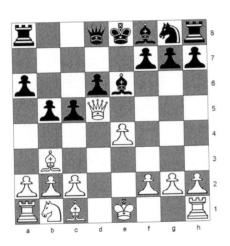

Noah's ark trap

1.e4 e5 2.Nf3 Nc6 3.Bb5
a6 4.Ba4 d6 5.d4?! (5. c3
is the main line) b5 6.Bb3
Nxd4 7.Nxd4 exd4
8.Qxd4 c5 9.Qd5 Be6!
followed by 10...c4
trapping and winning
the bishop

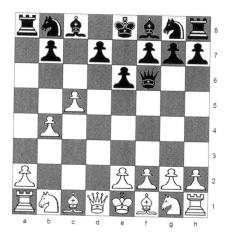

Old Benoni trap

1.d4 c5 2.dxc5 e6 3.b4 a5
4.c3 axb4 5.cxb4 Qf6
-+ traps the a1 rook

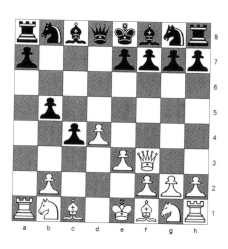

QGD trap

1.d4 d5 2.c4 dxc4 3.e3 b5
4.a4 c6 5.axb5 cxb5
6.Qf3+- traps the a8 rook

The good thing about openings is that the main lines do not change that quickly and only after many years do people find new ways of approaching certain openings. The only thing that changes quickly is chess players' preferences for certain openings!

Here are some recommended opening books:

Fundamental Chess Openings (2013) by Paul van der Sterren – an excellent book on understanding chess openings, their ideas, plans and fills in the gaps of Understanding the Chess Openings by Sam Collins

Understanding the Chess Openings (2005) by Sam Collins – a good overview of all major openings and explanation of some plans

Winning Chess Traps: Opening Tactics for the Advanced Beginner and Intermediate Player (2007) by Robert Snyder – if you are interested in learning more about opening traps, then this is a good book

Middlegame

The middlegame. This is what separates the good from the great. Anyone can memorise opening lines and opening traps, and endgame mastery is almost purely technical and can be learnt over time. The middlegame however, is where the artistry of chess lies and this is the chance for you show others how good of a player you really are and how well you understand chess positions.

In my opinion, how you should approach the middlegame is based on general strategies, the type of opening you play and the type of player you are.

General strategies

Develop quickly, control the centre (directly or indirectly), don't waste time (eg. move the same piece more than once, don't move your queen out too early, pawn grabbing etc.), get your king to safety, create mini-plans to achieve some major goal.

These are some of the strategies to keep in mind

For example, if you develop quickly in the opening, control the centre and have a safe king, you'll have more chances or opportunities to make a break in the centre to gain space, to gain space in the flanks, to attack a less developed and coordinated army, to attack a less well defended enemy king and so on. You can choose to do either or all of these strategies where possible.

How you approach the middlegame also depends largely on the opening you choose. For example, if you prefer to play a sharp, tactical game, then opening with the Sicilian Dragon or Open Spanish is a good way to start. If you prefer to a more solid game, then the QGD or the French Defence is your best bet. In general, king pawn openings (1. e4) are more tactical whereas queen pawn openings (1. d4) are more solid and positional.

You can get a rough idea as to who is better in a position by counting the number of points they've captured. Refer to the point chart in The Basic Rules chapter. This is actually more important than the amount of material you've captured by your side. As GM Alexei Shirov, once said, "pieces play chess". However, in reality, the player who has the advantage depends on the coordination and effectiveness of their pieces as well as the relative safety of their king.

You may also have heard about how important pawns are in chess. True, Francois Philidor, a very well-known chess player of the 18th century, once said "pawns are the soul of chess." However, is **pawn structure** really that important? It turns out that the answer to this question really depends on what type of position you're playing. Certain traditional weaknesses, like doubled-pawns and isolated pawns, can sometimes be useful to have either to bolster defence or to open up lines for attack.

Although pawns are the weakest unit, they are excellent defenders, cost-effective attackers, and can promote to any piece. Their coordination and positioning often influences how well your pieces move and thus how much you can control the board.

If you would like to learn more about pawn structure, then you can have a read of GM Andy Soltis' book Pawn Structure Chess (2013). Learning some opening traps will help you learn to avoid these, as well as be able to set them up against opponents. Although you shouldn't count on them since most decent players will not fall for them. Reserve these traps when you play blitz or very fast time limits; they often work better under these time conditions.

No one can read minds, unless you are truly psychic, so it's no surprise that you can't really predict what your opponent is going to do. However, you can **anticipate** what they can do and **be prepared** for these options. This is how you should really think when playing chess.

Forcing an opponents' moves in the middlegame is generally not a good idea. Beginners often make that mistake. Whilst many tactics have forceful combinations, the middlegame is not a purely tactical exercise. It is also strategic and positional, and you must learn how to understand these positions and have a 'feel' for them. It's not something that can be taught but after much practice you can achieve it.

There is 1 middlegame book that I can recommend and that is
Understanding Chess Middlegames (2013) by John Nunn

Planning an attack

Before launching an attack, you must make sure that your king is
safe, eg. There are no back rank tricks in the air and that your pieces
are well developed enough to attack as well as being able to retreat
for defence if necessary.

When you have spotted a weakness in the enemy position, you
have a target to attack.

Think to yourself, "Is there a weak square that I can take over? Are
there are weak pawns or badly positioned pieces that I can target?
Can I directly assault the enemy king?"

If you can say 'yes' to at least 1 of these questions, then you can
begin a plan of attack.

In the case of no obvious weaknesses, think about if there are any
breakthroughs in the centre, the king side or queen side or any piece
sacrifices.

In chess, there is usually more than 1 plan that is acceptable to play
so don't be worried about getting a concrete or exact answer. It's
better to have a lousy plan than to have no plan at all.

Here are some puzzles to help you learn to plan:

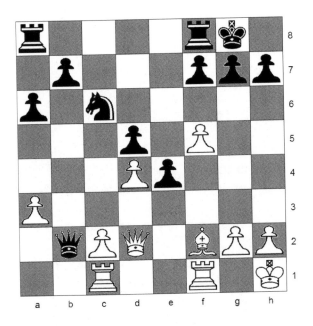

1. White to move

White's queenside has been breached by the black queen and it looks like a-pawn is about to fall as well, unless white decides to defend it with 1. Ra1. However, white's f-pawn is on the doorstep of black's king and the white queen isn't too far away from being able to attack black's king either. What could white play here?

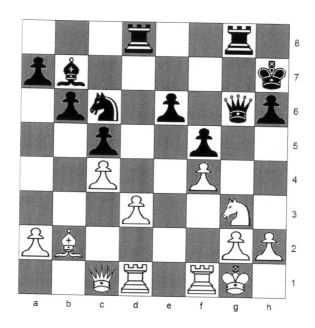

2. Black to move

White's king is looks deceptively safe but once the knight on g3 moves black can deliver checkmate on g2 with his queen. What can black play here?

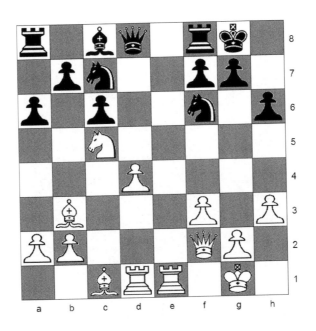

3. White to move

A good example of an isolated queen pawn position (also known as an IQP position). In such positions, the player with the isolated pawn, in this case white, is the attacker and black is the defender. This is because an isolated pawn is a weakness and white must attack in order to compensate for this weakness, otherwise black's slightly better pawn structure will allow him to easily take the advantage. Also having an isolated pawn means more open or semi-open lines that the attacker can play on, so it makes more sense for white to attack rather than to defend.

In any case, the position here looks like White is a little better here. White's pieces are well developed, the knight on c5 looks strong, the bishops are excellently positioned – pointing directly at black's kingside from a distance, the rooks occupy the central files and the king is safe. On the other hand, black is slightly under developed, the knight on c7 is awkwardly placed and aside from having control of the d5 square, there isn't that much going on for black.

So what can white do here?

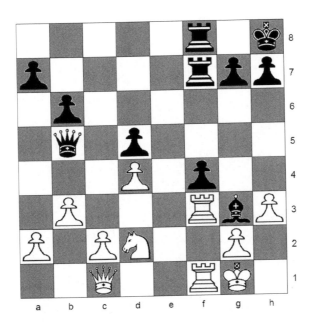

4. White to move

Black has a powerful bishop wedged near white's king on g3 and is causing issues for white to coordinate his pieces. What can white do to get out of this slightly worse position?

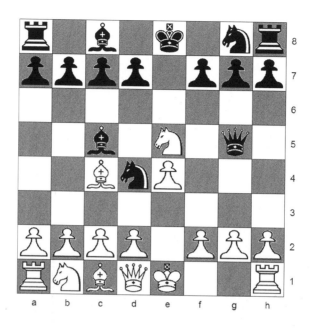

5. White to move

It's only the 6th move of the game but white is already in some
danger. The knight on e5 and the g2 pawn are under attack. If white
decides to be a bit greedy, it might cost him the game. What are
some variations here?

Tactics

Teichmann, a german master in the early 19th century, once said that "chess is 99% tactics". Clearly an exaggeration, but in some ways, he is right – you need to be able to calculate tactical combinations carefully, no matter what style of player you are. Simply put, tactics are like the bread and butter of chess, is what I would say.

You might go through these puzzles and think, this looks very similar to the planning puzzles since it's just a random chess position and then I have to solve it right? Well, not exactly. With planning, there isn't always a right or wrong answer, just that some answers may be better than others. However, with tactics, there is almost always a concrete answer.

I will give you some examples of what some tactical puzzles look like and their solutions:

<u>Example 1</u>

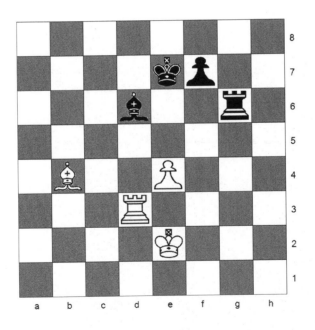

Black's bishop looks to be in serious danger but if the bishops are exchanged (1. Bxd6+, Rxd6), then the game will very likely end in a draw. However, white has a sneaky tricky up his sleeve …

1.Rxd6! (a good move that forces black to take back with the rook, otherwise he'll just be a bishop down for nothing) Rxd6 2.e5! (this move exploits the fact that black has pinned himself by taking back with the rook. Black can play any legal move here and white will simply take the rook with the pawn, leaving white a piece up and a winning endgame)
It's a good thing that the bishops weren't exchanged otherwise this trick wouldn't have been possible.

Here's another slightly harder example,

Example 2

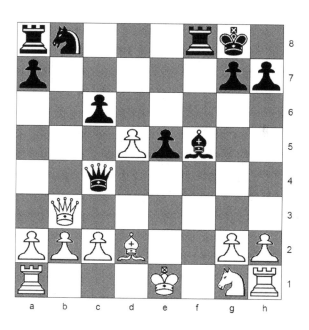

Black to move & win

Although a pawn up, white has pretty much lost the control of the centre and is also behind in development with the king still stuck in the centre. To make matters worse, it also black to move. Black could just take the pawn on d5 with his c-pawn and gain complete control of the centre with 2 connected passed pawns, but there is even a better move. In fact, it leads to checkmate in 3!

1... Qf1+!! (black sacrifices his queen in a forced combination) 2. Kxf1, Bd3++! (a discovered and double check by the rook on f8 and the bishop on d3 – a very lethal move indeed) 3. Ke1, Rf1# (and the white king has nowhere to run)

So here are some tactical problems to flex that chess brain of yours:

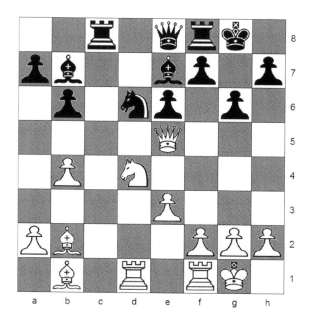

1. White to move & win

White's queen is strong in the centre and the dark squares around black's king are weak. It's only a matter of time before white crashes through.

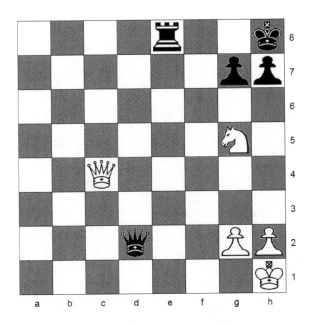

2. White to move and win

On first glance, it looks like black is winning since he is up an exchange, attacking white's knight and is about to mate white on the back rank (aka back rank mate) with 1...Re1+. However, it is white who strikes first and turns the tables around!

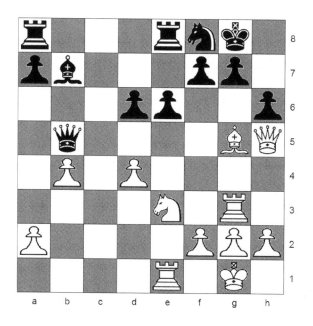

3. White to move and win

White looks like he's in trouble. His bishop is under attack and if it moves, then white's undefended queen will be ready to be taken by black's queen. So this puts white in a real dilemma ... or does it?

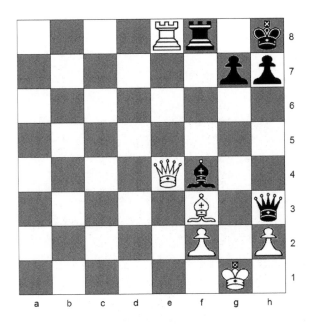

4. Black to move and win

Black looks like he is about to get mated on the back rank. On the other hand, white's king is fairly exposed and if black can somehow find a way to exploit this, he might just save, and even win the game.

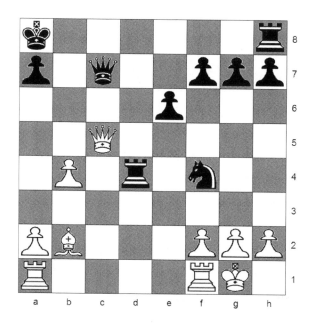

5. Black to move and win

Black's rook is under attack twice and white could win the pawn on g7 if the black rook on d4 decided to move out of the way.

However, it is white who should aware of the danger ahead and not black.

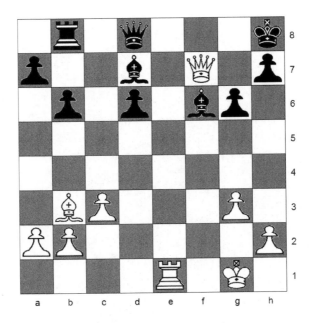

6. White to move and win

White is down a full piece but his queen is dangerously close to black's king. If there was a need for white to do something in order to not lose the game, it should be now.

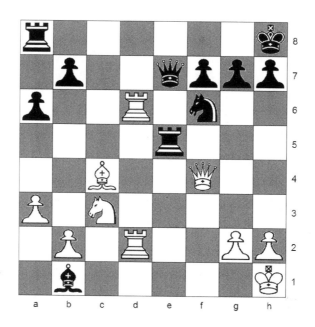

7. Black to move and win

A complex position with many things happening. Black is up 1 pawn but whites' pieces seem more coordinated. The only major concern for white would be his back rank as it looks a little vulnerable at the moment. Is there a way for black to exploit this?

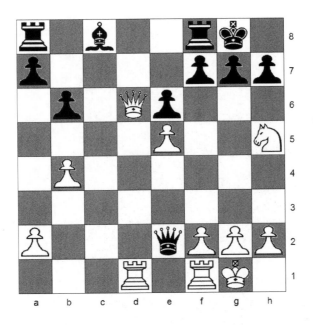

8. White to move and win

Right now, white controls more of the board than black does, although his knight on h5 is under attack. It seems that black's king is fairly safe and there are no back rank tricks just yet. But white does have a winning plan …

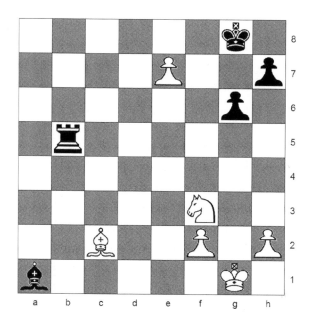

9. Black to move and draw

White's passed pawn is 1 step away from promotion and there is little that black and do to stop it, even though he is an exchange up. Black also must be careful of some traps lingering in the air because of this passed pawn. So what to do for black?

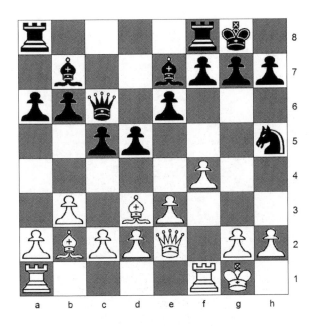

10. White to move and win

Whites' bishops actively placed and pointed directly at black's king. What can white do to shatter black's kingside and have a winning position?

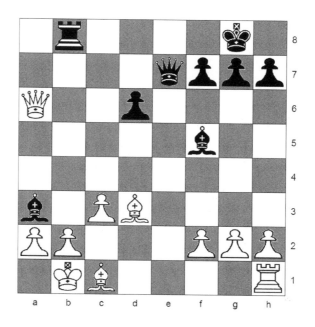

11. Black to move and win

White is under serious pressure here and the white kings' defence is on the verge of collapsing. Can black just put little more pressure on white's house of cards?

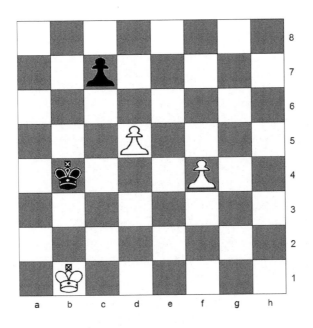

12. White to move and win

Does white's extra pawn count for something or can black hold them both off?

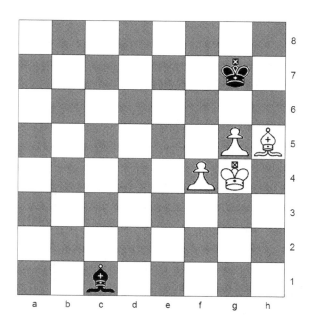

13. Black to move and draw

It seems like there's nothing that black can do to stop both of white's connected passed pawns. Or is there?

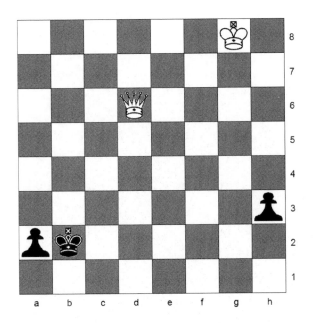

14. White to move and win

White appears to have an overwhelming advantage. 2 pawns stand no chance against a queen (usually). But 2 pawns that are close to promotion might be somewhat of a challenge. Can white actually win this endgame?

Now for the final tactical puzzle, let's finish this off with a bang shall we?

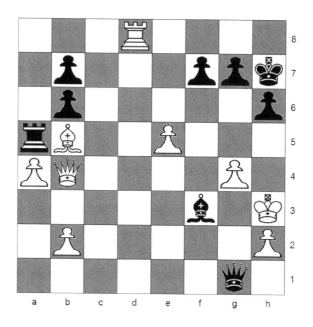

15. White to move and win

White's king looks really exposed and is in fact about to be mated 2 by black. Black's king, on the other hand looks fairly safe and his position is OK overall, aside from the oddly placed rook. What can White do here?

Magnus Carlsen, the current no 1 player in the world is probably one of the most talented middlegame players right now as he often diverges from mainline theory and tries to outplay weaker opponents on unknown territory. Not a bad strategy in itself ay?

Some recommended books to help you train your tactics are:
1001 Winning Chess Sacrifices and Combinations (2014) by Fred Reinfeld
Practical Chess Exercises (2007) by Ray Cheng – this has some positional exercises as well as tactical exercises
Chess: 5334 Problems, Combinations and Games (2013) by Laszlo Polgar – the title says it all

Endgame

The final phase of the game of chess and this is where you get to show off your technique. Most players count on outplaying their opponents in the middlegame stage so that they don't have to rely much on endgame technique. In reality, these players fall short in the endgame since endgame technique takes a fair amount of time and effort to learn. But learning the technique is quite important especially against players of a similar playing strength to you or above.

As a beginner, you'll want to know the basic endgame strategies. I'll list them below:

<u>Passed pawn</u> – a pawn with no opposing pawn on the same file or the files adjacent to it i.e. a pawn that cannot be stopped by an opponents' pawns

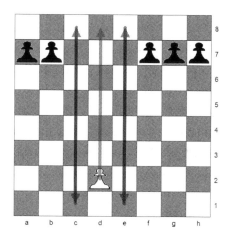

<u>Square of the pawn</u> – an imaginary square that allows the king to be able catch up to a passed pawn.

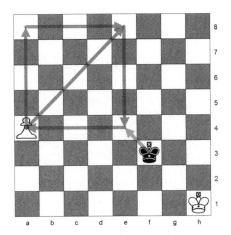

The square of the pawn is drawn by drawing a diagonal from the pawn to the back rank (from a4 to e8) and then completing a square from that diagonal (e8-e4-a4-a8-e8).

If it is Black's turn to move, then Black could play Ke4 and enter the square of the pawn, which would allow Black to capture the passed pawn on time. If it is White's turn to move, however, then White would be able to promote the pawn since Black's king would not be able to catch it on time.

Triangulation – a technique that repeats the same position but "passes" the move onto the opponent. This is the closest thing to passing a move in chess. Here is an example,

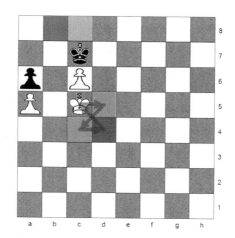

It is White's turn to move. If White tries to promote the c-pawn directly, then Black can reach a stalemate position, for example, 1. Kd5, Kc8 2. Kd6, Kd8 3. c7+, Kc8 4. Kc6=. So instead, White uses triangulation in order to "lose a move", because if it Black were to move in this position, then White would simply play Kb6, win the a-pawn, and Black wouldn't be able to stop both pawns.

1. Kd5, Kc8 2. Kc4!, Kb8 3. Kd4!, Kc7 4. Kc5 and now the starting position has been reached but with Black to move, Kb8 5. Kb6 and white wins easily.

<u>Opposition</u> – a zugzwang position created by kings separated by an odd number of squares, either horizontally or vertically

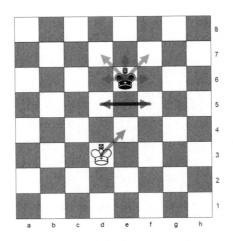

If white plays Ke4, white will "gain the opposition" and force black to move side to side or backwards.

In diagram on the right, if white plays Ke1, then white is also said to have gained the opposition ("distant opposition")

There is such a thing as "diagonal opposition", but it will not be covered in this book.

<u>Shouldering</u> – this is a king move that forces the enemy king to move elsewhere due to opposition. Shouldering is really an effect of using opposition multiple times.

<u>Wrong colored bishop</u> – refers to a bishop that cannot help a passed rook pawn to promote and 90% of the time will end in a draw.

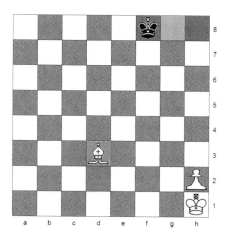

In the diagram above, if Black keeps the king along the green colored squares, then he can pretty much guarantee a drawn game. Notice the different colored square of the bishop (d3) compared with the promotion square of the pawn (h8).

Just for your interest, here is how you can win this endgame

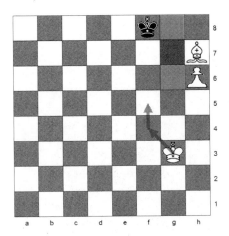

You create this setup with the bishop and pawn. The stronger side's king, in this case white, must be close enough to the bishop and pawn in order to shoulder black's king away from the pawn. Once that is done, simply promote the pawn and win.

Stalemate or Drawing Tricks

This occurs often in endgames and is useful if you are losing and need to save the game. Here is one example:

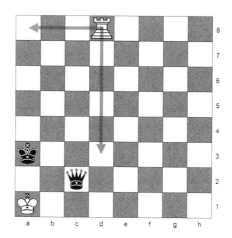

In this position, white can play 1. Ra8+ or 1. Rd3+ to save the game. For example, 1. Ra8+, Kb4 2. Rb8+, Ka5 3. Ra8+, Kb6 4. Rb8+, Ka7 5. Ra8+!, Kxa8= stalemate. The king can't cross the c-file otherwise Rc8+! will force black to take the rook and stalemate the white king anyway.

Also 1. Rd3+, Kb4 (1…Qxd3= stalemate) 2. Rd4+, Kc5 (2…Kc3 3. Rc4+!=) 3. Rd5+!= will eventually lead to perpetual check or stalemate.

<u>Perpetual check</u> – a situation where the check can be delivered consecutively and the player being checked is unable to prevent the checks.

This is shown in the previous position about stalemate tricks. Perpetual check can occur at any phase of the game, whereas stalemate very rarely occurs in the opening or middlegame. Here is an example:

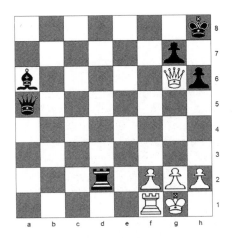

White is down a piece and trying to win this game for white is impractical. In this position, a draw is more than sufficient.
1.Qe8+ Kh7 2.Qe4+ Kg8 3.Qe8+ Kh7 4.Qe4+ g6 5.Qe7+ Kg8 6.Qe8+ Kg7 7.Qe7+ Kg8 8.Qe8+ Kh7 9.Qe7+ Kh8= and the players agreed to a draw.
*As a side note, FIDE (pronounced 'fee-day'), the international federation of chess, removed perpetual check as a rule of chess sometime in 2011 since it basically leads to a draw by agreement, 3 fold repetition or the 50 move rule.

50 move rule – a rule that states that if there is no pawn movement or capture within 50 moves, then the player making the move can claim a draw.
3 fold repetition – a rule that states that if the same position occurs at least 3 times in a game, then the player making the move can claim a draw. The move order is irrelevant.

Harder Endgame Positions

Here are some harder endgame positions

K & Q v. K & N or B – the strategy is to eliminate either the bishop
or knight then proceed to checkmate. The only thing to be careful
about are forks from the knight and pins or skewers from the
bishop

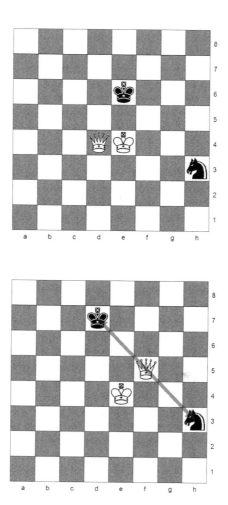

1.Qe5+ Kd7 2.Qf5+ and then followed by Qxh3. The rest is simple.

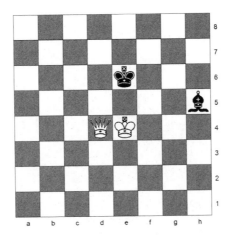

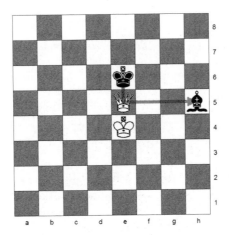

Or with a bishop,

1.Qe5+ followed by Qxh5. The rest is simple. In general, playing against a bishop is easier than the knight because the bishop is limited to one square color. So instead of trying to capture the piece, you can just play on the opposite color squares of the bishop and win by doing that instead.

K & Q v. K & R – the strategy is to also eliminate the rook and then proceed to checkmate. However, this is easier said than done and even grandmasters have a hard time doing this. One basic position to remember is the Philidor position shown below. It is white to move here.

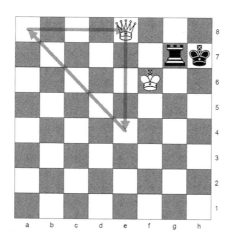

This position relies on a technique called triangulation, which as you know by now, places the weaker side in zugzwang and allows you to win by force. Here are the variations:

1. Qe4+, Kg8 2. Qa8+, Kh7 3. Qe8! (triangulation)
(3...Rg1 4. Qe4+, Kg8 {4...Kh8 5. Qa8+, Rg8 6. Qh1#} 5. Qa8+, Kh7 6. Qa7+)
(3...Rc7 4. Qe4+, Kg8 5. Qd5+ {5...Kf8 6. Qd8#}, Kh7 6. Qd3+ {6...Kh6 7. Qh3#}, Kh8 7. Qd8+)
(3...Rb7 4. Qe4+)
(3...Rg4 4. Qh5+)
(3...Rg3 4. Qe4+, Kg8 {4...Kh8 5. Qh4+} 5. Qc4+, Kh7 6. Qh4+ or Qc7+)
(3...Rg2 4. Qe4+)
 (3...Kh6 4. Qc8)
3... Ra7 4. Qh5+, Kg8 5. Qd5+, Kh7 {5...Kf8 6.Qd8# or 5...Kh8 6. Qh1+, Rh7 7. Qa8#} 6. Qh1+, Kg8 7. Qg1+
In all these variations, white forks the king and rook or gets checkmate.

You don't need to know this off by heart, just the idea of triangulation and how it can be used to your advantage.

There are in fact many ideas and tricks in this relatively basic endgame but these are quite complicated and far beyond the scope of this book.

If you'd like more information, you can check out this Chess Endgames 3: Major Piece Endgames (software) by Karsten Muller or Secrets of Pawnless Endings: An Expanded Edition of a Ground-Breaking Work by John Nunn.

K & R v. K & N – the strategy is once again to eliminate the knight and deliver checkmate. The rook, combined with the king, should be able to trap the knight. Watch out for forks though.

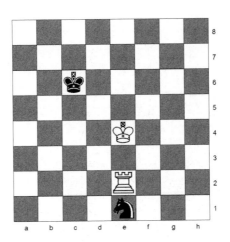

Trapping the knight

K & R v. K & B – the strategy is to eliminate the bishop and deliver checkmate. The rook and king will not be able to trap the bishop but by pushing the enemy king into the "right" corner of the bishop and creating mate threats, this endgame should be winnable (although harder than K & R v. K & N). Watch out for pins and skewers.

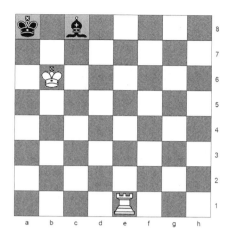

The black king in the "right" corner of the bishop. This is an easy win, for example 1.Re8 Kb8 2.Rd8 (zugzwang) Ka8 3.Rxc8#

K & Q v. K & P (2nd rank black pawn or 7th rank white pawn) – the strategy is to eliminate the pawn and deliver checkmate. The general rule is that centre and knight pawns are won, whereas rook and bishop pawns are drawn positions. However, this isn't always the case.

White can win in the following positions:

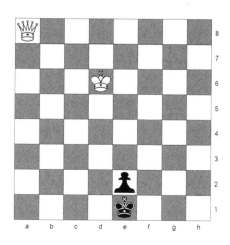

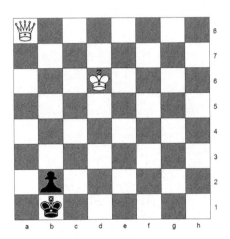

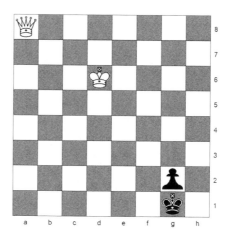

The following positions are drawn (with best play):

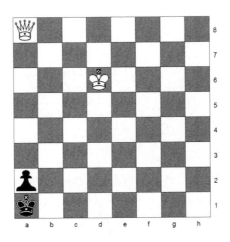

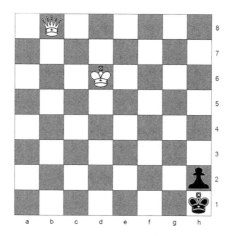

Note: the queen's position (within reason) does not affect the outcome of this endgame

There are some circumstances where it is possible to win against a rook or bishop pawn. This is only possible if the **stronger side's king is close enough to the weaker side's king**. For example,

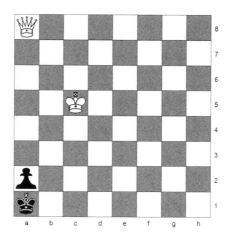

In the drawn position with the a-pawn, if the king was on c5 instead of d6, then white can in fact win! For example, 1.Kb4 Kb2 2.Qg2+ Kb1 3.Kb3 (3... a1=Q 4.Qg1#), a1=N+ 4. Kc3 and white has mate in 2 more moves (Qxc2+ then Qb2#)

In these positions, if the black pawn isn't on the 2nd rank (or 7th rank white pawn for black), then white can win against any pawn since white could simply blockade any square leading to promotion by the pawn with the queen. Of course, we're making the assumption that white (or black) can actually blockade any of those squares with the queen on time.

For instance, in the above position, if the black pawn was on the 3rd rank and the white king was on d6 and it was black to move, then the position would be a draw (the position transposes into one of the drawn examples)

So in summary, the win is only difficult (if not impossible) if the pawn is about to be promoted.

Rook pawns in general aren't very good in helping the stronger side win in the endgame. This is because they are at the edge of the board and there is less manoeuvrability there for your pieces to help guide it safely to promotion. There are some instances when you can win with rook pawns but it requires great technique and precision. From a practical point of view, it is easier just to take a draw.

Another saying you might hear as a beginner is that "all rook endgames are drawn". This refers to K & (R or 2R) + (any number of pawns) v. K & (R or 2R) + (similar number of pawns). Of course, this is an exaggeration but it simply means that these sorts of positions tend to end in draws. However, if the **stronger side is at least 2 pawns up in material, then the chances of winning are much higher.**

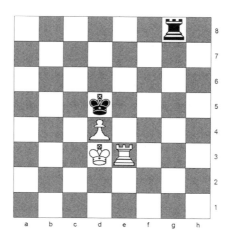

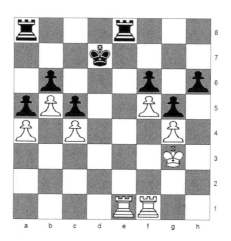

It is very likely that these positions will end in a draw despite one side having an extra pawn.

One phrase you might hear is "insufficient mating material". The most obvious example is a position with just a white and black king left on the board. This means that either (or in this case, both) sides do not have enough material to deliver checkmate and is by default a draw. Other examples include K & N v. K, K & B v. K and K & 2N v. K etc.

A great endgame book for beginners is Pandolfini's Endgame Course: Basic Endgame Concepts Explained by America's Leading Chess Teacher. It shows you some key endgame positions and explains what you should do. Highly recommended.

Practical Chess Tips

By now, you can tell that there is a lot to learn about chess. Depending on your motivation, it'll take at least 1 to 2 years to become a reasonably good player (when I mean good, I mean a club level player ELO 1600 – 1800). If you're thinking of becoming a master level player, which is ELO 2300 and beyond, you will need to take chess seriously and spend at least 3 hours studying & playing chess every day.

However, there are certain things that good players always keep in mind and this definitely helps you win more games, reduce your losses and ultimately helps you improve faster.

(ELO – an international rating for chess. It indicates how strong of a player you are – the higher the number, the better you are theoretically)

Here are some practical tips for playing chess:

Play the moves out on a board – when you're just starting out, you're probably not going to be able to remember many moves in your head. It's a good idea to have a chess set with you, whether it's a physical chess set that you can touch or with a chess program because this will help you see the moves more clearly and understand the ideas behind certain combinations or plans.

Know at least 1 opening very well, preferably a lesser known opening – your opponents may eventually be able to predict your moves easier and prepare against you, but it's better to play what you're comfortable with. Also, you're not likely to be playing against grandmasters so you can afford to play sidelines and also get away with minor inaccuracies.

Watch the clock – there are some players who simply take too much time on the clock and end up losing because of being "flagged" (another term for losing on time). It's best that you play safe, sensible moves, instead of always trying to find some highly sophisticated tactical shot that will end the game in 16 moves by force, simply because you won't have the time in the end. This is especially true in blitz games

Focus – if you've ever played in tournaments, you may see some players get out of their seat to watch other games. This is good for bodily circulation as well as just relaxing your mind from the mental challenges posed in your game. However, it is very easy to lose focus and make a huge mistake when you return to your board, so be mindful when you find yourself relaxing too much!

Keep a lookout for intermediate (in-between) moves – being able to use intermediate moves won't necessarily win you the game, but it is often quite surprising to an opponent, simply because it's a move they won't really expect. These kinds of moves are great for setting up tactics or getting out of trouble. Due to its surprise element, it can give you a psychological edge since it disrupts the rhythm of your opponent. Just don't go checking your opponent to death because it might lead to a perpetual.

Think about move order – sometimes, certain tactics don't work because you've calculated them in the wrong move order.

Plan, plan, plan – one of the most well renowned world chess champions, Mikhail Botvinnik, taught his students to always plan, even in blitz games. It might be daunting at first to always have to think of so many options, but it will train you to be thinking on the right path and eventually, this will become second nature to you to the point where you won't even have to consciously plan at all.

Above all else, the greatest advice I can give you is to practise playing chess with all kinds of people. If you're just a beginner, play against someone who is also a beginner or slightly better than you. Chess is after all, a contest between 2 players and simply reading books or even playing against the computer will only be so much. Humans play differently to computers and you'll also be able to try out different openings and strategies with human players, more so than computers. Also, it will be nice to be able to talk during a friendly game, as opposing to staring into a voiceless computer screen.

Chess from Now to Beyond

Chess has been played for thousands of years and it looks like it'll stay that way for many more years to come. Even if computers manage to fully work out chess, the game itself is still a great way to keep your mind active and meet like-minded people.

The Chess Olympiad held this year was a great success with a record of nearly 2000 players from about 180 countries around the world. China was the winner in the open section and the team only lost 1 game throughout the entire tournament!

The current world chess champion, Magnus Carlsen, is also the world rapid and blitz champion. He is the first and only person so far to have won all three titles!

The upcoming world chess championship in November this year, which will take place in Russia, sees Magnus Carlsen, the current world champion, take on former 5-time world champion Viswanathan Anand. In fact, last year, it was Viswanathan Anand who was world champion so this upcoming championship is almost like a "revenge rematch" of last year.

Many fans were surprised that Anand (as he is better known as), was able to win the Candidates tournament and qualify to become the challenger due to his relatively old age of 44 and that there were other likely candidates like Levon Aronian and Vladimir Kramnik. Nevertheless, this upcoming world chess championship will also promise to be an exciting one and it could really go either way. Will it be the Norweigan wunderkind to add yet another trophy to his already overloaded trophy cabinet or will it be the Bengal tiger who will claw his way back in and take everyone by surprise? Only time will tell.

As you can see, many exciting things are happening in 2014 for chess at the moment. I guess it's time you pick up the pieces and join in with the battle. As Bobby Fischer once said "I leave this to you".

Recommended Resources

www.chessblog.info – Visit this site to learn more about chess and maybe even the author of this book

www.fide.com – the International Federation of Chess website

www.chessbase.com – up to date chess news around the world

www.chess.com – a good place to play chess online, geared towards beginners

www.chessclub.com (aka ICC) – the number 1 place to play chess online, geared towards club level players and beyond, sign up today

https://www.youtube.com/channel/UCM-ONC2bCHytG2mYtKDmIeA - the Chess Club and Scholastic Center of St. Louis youtube channel. It has many great chess related videos, especially the lectures that average around 40 minutes each

Your local chess club site, state/national website, for example

www.auschess.org.au Australian Chess Federation

www.englishchess.org.uk English Chess Federation

www.uschess.org United States Chess Federation

Chess forums like www.chessforums.org and www.chessbanter.com are a good place to talk with other players about chess amongst other things

Any nearby chess clubs where you can play against real people

www.chesstempo.com – a tactics training site. Be wary that some of the puzzles are very difficult so get too discouraged if you can't seem to get any of them right

Chess books – you don't need many just, a few on tactics, an opening, a strategy one and an endgame one to start off. I find that chess books are generally written in an easier to follow manner compared to online material.

Chessbase software – This software allows you to store your games and analyze them with a computer (virtually all Chessbase software has a built-in chess engine). It is used by chess professionals around the world and is the gold standard. Highly recommended.

The latest version is Chessbase 12. You can get it here.

Chess playing programs – About a decade ago, Chessmaster was very popular, user friendly and the general population seemed to like it. However, it was not a particularly strong program compared with several others, like Fritz, Rybka, Houdini or more recently Komodo.

As a beginner, Chessmaster will suit all your needs as a chess playing program

Answers

Quick quiz – the king
Answer: 5

K & 2R v. K question
Answer: 1. Rb1, Ka4 2. Ra2# (in this case, cutting the king off by file
is faster)

K & N + B v. K practice position
Answer: Either to a1 or h8

<u>Planning</u>
Puzzle 1

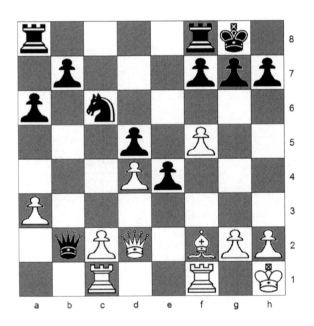

White could play 1. f6 offering to sacrifice the f-pawn in order to open up attacking lines towards the black king. For example, if 1…gxf6, then 2. Qh6 planning to play Bh4, Bxf6 then Qg7#. Black can respond with 2…Re8 but white can still continue with 3. Bh4, Re6 4. Bxf6, Rxf6 (the only way to stop mate) 5. Qxf6 and white is up a clear exchange with an attack. Black certainly can't afford to be greedy with 2…Nxd4 because then the Bh4 plan will work even better. For example, 3. Bh4, Ne6 (defending the g7 square, however) 4. Bxf6, Qxa3 5. Rf5 and the threat of Rg5+ followed by Qg7+ is completely winning.

Black can decline the pawn sacrifice either by ignoring the pawn or moving his g-pawn. Moving the g-pawn is disastrous for black since it will be impossible to stop checkmate on g7 by Qh6 and then Qg7#. If black plays 1…Qxa3 then simply 2. Qg5 is winning followed by Qh6 and then mate on g7 again. If black plays 1…h6 in order to stop Qg5 then white just takes on g7, then play Be3 and then double the rooks on the f-file eg. Rf5 followed by Rcf1 with a crushing attack on the king.

Puzzle 2

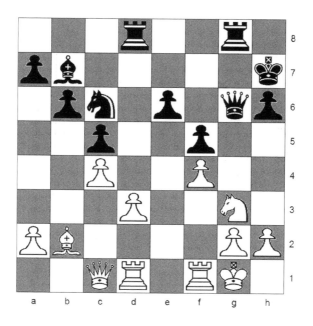

One possible move is 1...h5 planning to force the knight to move with 2...h4. White can't play h4 himself to stop black from playing h4 because then the knight on g3 will be hanging (the chess term meaning undefended) and black simply takes it for free with the queen. White can anticipate black's move and play 2. Rf2 to defend g2 and then 2...h4 3. Nf1, Nb4! threatening to take on d3 with the knight and fork the white queen and rook on f2 as well as to create a discovery attack onto g2 by the bishop on b7.

No matter what white does, black will able to get an advantage. For example, 4. Rfd2?? (protecting the d3 pawn and preventing the fork), Qxg2+!! 5. Rxg2, Rxg2+ 6. Rg3# (it's a "discovered mate" since amazingly, white cannot block the bishop along the a8-h1 diagonal)

Notice how awkward white's knight is placed. If the knight wasn't on f1, then white's king could've escaped to f1 and not get mated. But then again, it was awkwardly placed on g3 to begin with and f1 was, in fact, the best square for the knight at that time. Just something to keep in mind.

If white doesn't defend on d3 and plays 4. Ne3 to defend on g2 and help the white king escape from mate, then black simply plays 4...Nxd3 and wins a clear exchange.

Puzzle 3

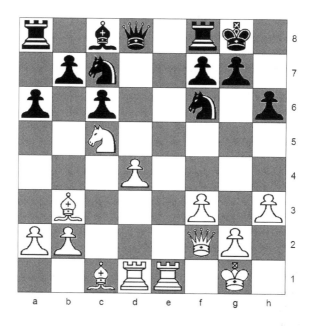

White can play 1. Qg3 threatening to take on h6 with the bishop on c1, and in doing so, threaten checkmate on g7. Black could simply move the king out the potential pin by playing 1...Kh7 (or 1...Kh8) 2. Bf4 (simple development), Ncd5 (if 2...Nh5 then 3. Bxc7!, Nxg3 4. Bxd8, Rxd8 5. Bxf7 and white is up a pawn) 3. Be5 (centralising the bishop), Nh5 4. Qf2, Nhf4 (supporting the knight on d5 and maybe planning some kingside attack later on) 5. Ne4 (repositioning the knight back onto the centre). While blacks' pieces are becoming more active, white maintains his slight advantage due to his centralised pieces controlling more space than black.

You can skip this part if you like [This is a little more advanced for beginners but a good plan from here, would be to drop the light-squared bishop to c2 and start advancing the queenside pawns to start a minority attack with a4, b4, b5, at the right time of course. This is called a **minority attack because white has less queenside pawns than black but is initiating an attack despite this. This attack will help open up black's queenside in order for white to infiltrate with his rooks and increase his advantage.]

Other moves by black to stop the checkmate will lead to a worse position for black. For example, if 1...g6 then 2. Qxg6+! (black can't take the queen because the f7 pawn is pinned by the bishop on b3) and white completely breaks open the black king's Defence. If 1...g5 then 2. h4 will be winning for white. For example, 2...Nh5 3. Qh2, Ng7 4. hxg4, hxg4 5. Qh6 and white threatens Bxg5, Bf6 and Qxg7#. If black plays 1...Nh5 attacking the queen and defending g7 then white plays 2. Qg6! again (the f7 pawn is pinned) . Now, black's knight is under attack as well as Bxh6, Qxg7# is being threatened. White is simply winning.

Sometimes the simple moves are the best moves in a position.

Puzzle 4

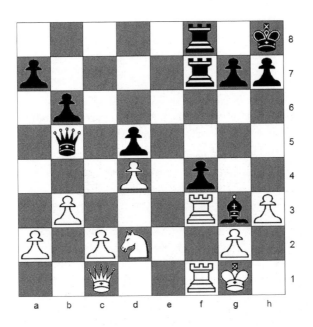

White can try 1. c4. If black takes the pawn with 1...dxc4 then 2. Ne4 followed by 3. Nxg3 will help free white from the bind he is in. For example, 2. Ne4, cxb3 3. Nxg3, bxa2 (if 3...fxg3?? then 4. Rxf7 wins a rook) 4. Rxf4, Rxf4 5. Rxf4, Kg8 (if 5...Rxf4 then 6. Qc8+ and white mates in 2 more moves) 6. Rxf8+, Kxf8 7. Qa3+ and white picks up the dangerous a-pawn and is up a piece in the end.

Instead of taking on c4, black is better off if he ignores the pawn and moves the queen back. White will then try to get his knight on e5 and that should balance up with black's strong bishop on g3. For example 1... Qc6 2. Rc3, dxc4 3. bxc4, Qd7 4. Rd3, Re8 (black plans to double on the e-file) 5. Nf3, Rfe7 6. Qc2 (white can't play 6. Ne5 straight away because 6...Rxe5! wins a piece for black due to the pin along the d-file), Re2 7. Rd2 then after the rooks are exchanged, white plays Ne5 and the position is about equal.

Puzzle 5

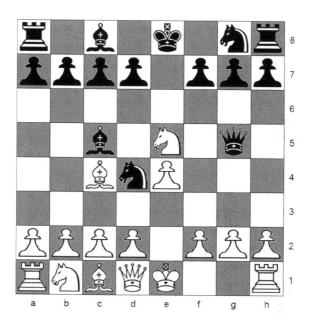

If white does decide to be greedy by playing 1. Nxf7 forking the queen and rook, then black continues with 1...Qxg2! 2. Rf1 if 2.Nxh8 then 2...Nf3+ 3. Ke2, Qxf2+ 4. Kd3 (the king is marching up the board ... to his doom), Ne5+ 5. Kc3, Qd4+ 6. Kb3, Qxc4# so instead white played 2. Rf1 then 2... Qe4+ 3. Be2 and then 3... Nf3# (smothered mate) This is what actually happened in the game.

However, white doesn't need to be greedy and immediately lose the game. Instead, white could've played 1. Bxf7+, Kf8 2. 0-0, Qxe5 3. Bxg8, Kxg8 4. c3, Bd6 5. f4, Qxe4 6. cxd4 and after Qxd4+ white will be down a pawn but black has lost castling rights so the position is about equal.

Another possibility is 1.0-0 immediately then 1...Qxe5 2. c3, Nc6 (if 2...Bd6 then 3. g3, Ne6 4. d4 and although white is a piece down, he can just simply push his pawns to gain tempo by harassing black's queen but at the same time gain space and develop quickly. Here's a sample line 4... Qa5 5. b4, Qb6 6. Be3, Nd8 7. d5, c5 8. e5, Bxe5 9. Re1, Qc7 10. f4, cxb4 11. Qd3, d6 12. dxe5, dxe5 13. cxb4, a6 14. Nc3 and white is slightly better) 3. d4, Nxd4 4. cxd4, Bxd4 5. Qb3. White is down 1 pawn but his king is safe and he can quickly develop his pieces by Nc3, Kh1, f4, Bd2, Rad1, whereas black has been too busy taking pawns and moving the queen too many times.

Tactics
Puzzle 1
1. Qg7+!! (in fact, he does it immediately!), Kxg7 2. Nf5++! (a deadly discovered double check yet again! The black king only has 1 square to move to.), Kg8 3. Nh6# (a picturesque mate)

Puzzle 2
1. Nf7+! (an innocent looking check with a potent venom), Kg8 2. Nh6++! (another check, but is it getting anywhere? Or is white just happy with a perpetual check?), Kh8 3. Qg8+!! (a bolt from the blue. Black must take the queen with the rook), Rxg8 4. Nf7#! (but it leads to checkmate, aka smothered mate since the king is smothered by his own army)

Puzzle 3

1. Bf6!! (white ignores his queen completely! Has he completely lost his mind!!), Qxh5 (the best move for black here) 2. Rxg7+! (this sets up a strategic device what some people call the 'windmill'), Kh8 3. Rxf7+ (discovered check! Black's king only has 1 square to go), Kg8 4. Rg7+ (the black king only has 1 square to go again), Rxb7+ (white is simply mopping up black's army on the 7th rank due to the windmill), Kg8 5. Rg7+ (white decides not to be too greedy), Kh8 (forced again) 6. Rg5+ (but white goes to collect the black queen after which he'll be 2 pawns and a piece up. A completely winning position for white)

Puzzle 4
1… Bxh2+!! (black completely ignores the threat on f8 and goes on to deliver mate himself!) 2. Kh1, Bg3+! (this sets up the mating net that black was hoping for) 3. Kg1, Qh2+ 4. Kf1, Qxf2# (a nice trick, don't you think?)

Puzzle 5
1…Ne2+! (another seemingly harmless check) 2. Kh1 (it looks like white's king is safe and sound), Qxh2+!! (not!!) 3. Kxh2, Rh4# (a nice looking mate. It is also known as Anastasia's mate named after a novel by a German author named Johann Heinse)

Puzzle 6
1.Re8+!! (a rook sacrifice that achieves 1 of 2 purposes. If black takes back with the queen, then the rook has deflected the queen from the Defence of the bishop on f6 and so 2. Qxf6# is in fact checkmate. Or, if black takes back with the bishop, then the rook has effectively forced the bishop to blockade the black queen from defending the g8 square and so 2. Qg8# is also checkmate. Simple but effective.)

Puzzle 7
1…Bd3!! (amazingly there is! Black deliberately places his bishop under a triple attack but no matter how white captures the bishop, black will end up ahead. For example, if either rook recaptures the bishop, then black plays 2…Re1+ followed by mate. If white captures the bishop with his bishop, then black simply plays 2…Qxd6 and be a clear exchange up. A hard move to find)

Puzzle 8
1. Nf6+!! (a totally unexpected move), gxf6 (forced, otherwise white will take the rook on f8 with mate) 2. exf6! (now black cannot escape mate. How you might ask? White is threatening 2 ways of checkmate. The first one is 3. Qxf8+!!, Kxf8 4. Rd8# and the other one is 3. Qg3+, Kh8 4. Qg7#. There is no way that black and defend against both at the same time so white will win this game)

Puzzle 9
1...Rb8! (the correct Defence. If 1...Kf7, then 2. e8=Q+!, Kxe8 3. Ba4 and white will win due to the pin) 2. Ba4, Kf7 (the pawn must be stopped) 3. e8=Q+, Rxe8 4. Ng5+, Kf6 5. Nxh7+, Kg7 6. Bxe8, Kxh7 and the opposite colored bishop endgame will likely end in a draw.

Puzzle 10
1. Bxh7+! (white sacrifices the bishop on d3, if black declines the sacrifice with 1...Kh8 then 2. Qxh5 is devastating for black), Kxh7 2. Qxh5+, Kg8 (the black king looks safe and there aren't any direct threats yet 3. Bxg7!! (a fantastic shot and offering to sacrifice the other bishop as well), Kxg7 (black must accept the sacrifice, otherwise white will have a crushing attack or checkmate) 4. Qg4+ (preventing the king from escaping. If 4...Kf6, then 5. Qg5#), Kh7 5. Rf3 (and it's curtains for black), e5 (the only move to stop mate) 6. Rh3+, Qh6 7. Rxh6+ and the rest is simple
A perfect example of the double bishop sacrifice motif.

Puzzle 11
1...Qe2!! (black is threatening to take on d3 with the bishop as well as taking on b2. Notice, white can't take the queen since the white d3 bishop is pinned) 2. Rd1 (the best Defence), Qxd1! (this is the correct winning move. There were other tempting options: 2...Rxb2+? 3. Ka1 and black has no mating threat. 2... Bxb2? threatening discovered check but 3. Qxd6 and the position is not so clear anymore since a discovered check by the by black can be met by the white queen taking the rook on b8)
If 3. Qxa3, then simply black takes the bishop on d3 and it's mate the next move after that. If 3. Bxf5, then 3...Rxb2# since the rook can't be taken due to the pin by the black queen.
A lot of pins in this one.